BRU

TRAVEL GUI

A Symphony of Sounds, Sights,

and Sensations

ALICE JOHN

Copyright ©2023 Alice John

All rights reserved. No portion of this work may be duplicated, saved in a database, or transmitted—electronic, mechanical, photocopying, recording, scanning, or any other method—without the author's prior written consent.

CONTENTS

INTRODUCTION 7

CHAPTER 1 9

BRIEF HISTORY OF BRUGES 9
LANGUAGE AND PHRASES 11
CHOOSING THE BEST TIME TO VISIT 15
TRAVEL ESSENTIALS 17
MAP OF BRUGGE 19

CHAPTER 2 20

GETTING AROUND 20
GETTING TO BRUGES 20
CULTURE & CUSTOMS 21
TIPS FOR TRAVELERS 21

CHAPTER 3 24

TOP ATTRACTIONS IN BRUGES 24
MUST-SEE ACTIVITIES 33

CHAPTER 4 38

HOTELS 38
RESTAURANTS 56

CHAPTER 5 67

3

TOP PERFECT SOUVENIRS IN BRUGES 67

CHRISTMAS ORNAMENTS 67
FLEMISH TAPESTRIES 68
COMIC BOOKS 68
CHOCOLATES 69
ANTIQUES 70
CHEESE 71
SWEETS 72
LACE 73

CHAPTER 6 74

MUST-VISIT EVENTS IN BRUGES 75
FIVE-DAY ITINERARY 76

CHAPTER 7 81

SAFETY AND SECURITY IN BRUGES 81

CONCLUSION 85

WELCOME TO BRUGES, BELGIUM

4

INTRODUCTION

Step into the enchanting city of Bruges, a captivating realm where medieval charm intertwines with modern vibrancy. Located in the heart of Northwest Belgium, Bruges, affectionately known as the "Pearl of Flanders," stands as a testament to time, where every cobblestone whisper tales of a splendid bygone era. As you step into this UNESCO World Heritage Site, you're whisked back to an age of knights, bustling markets, and artistic brilliance. The rhythmic clop of horse-drawn carriages guides you through narrow alleys, each weathered brick facade adorned with intricate lacework, murmuring secrets of Bruges' illustrious past. Imagine the city in its prime, a bustling hub where European traders brought spices from distant lands. Picture Markt Square as a vibrant tapestry of stalls laden with local treasures while the towering Belfort proudly presides over the lively scene. Take a serene canal cruise, gliding along tranquil waterways, mesmerized by the play of light on medieval architecture reflected in the shimmering waters. Enter the revered Church of Our Lady, where Michelangelo's Madonna and Child sculpture presides over exquisite Gothic wonders. Discover the vivid canvases of Flemish Primitives like Hans Memling and Jan van Eyck, telling tales of faith and humanity. Indulge in Flemish delights—rich stews, fresh seafood, and divine chocolates—each bite a symphony of flavors that ignites your senses. As evening descends, Bruges transforms into a magical wonderland, with lights adorning ancient streets. Cozy pubs resonate with laughter and the clinking of glasses, enveloping you in an atmosphere of warmth and conviviality. Bruges beckons, inviting you to explore its captivating essence, where history whispers and enchantment dances at every turn. Immerse yourself in its timeless allure, where past and present harmonize seamlessly, promising an unforgettable journey through the ages.

CHAPTER 1

Brief History of Bruges

Bruges, a mesmerizing city nestled in Belgium, unfurls a tapestry of history woven over centuries, starting its tale in the 9th century. Once a humble fishing village, it evolved into a bustling trading haven, witnessing an extraordinary metamorphosis through time.

Origins and Roman Influence

In the 9th century, Bruges emerged along the river Reie, gradually blossoming into a vibrant city by the 12th century. Positioned at the crossroads of vital trade routes, it swiftly became a bustling commercial hub, drawing merchants far and wide. Under Roman rule, around the 1st century BC, Bruges, known as "Britonia," flourished. The Romans engineered a canal connecting Bruges to the North Sea, further elevating its significance in trade.

The Flourishing Golden Age
Between the 12th and 15th centuries, Bruges witnessed its zenith, thriving as a commercial and cultural epicenter. Its prosperity stemmed from dominance in the cloth trade, particularly prized Flemish woolen textiles, coveted across Europe. This era birthed architectural wonders like the Belfry, the Church of Our Lady, and the Market Square. These landmarks, symbolic of opulence and achievement, endure as icons of Bruges' grandeur.

The Shifts and Renaissance
The 16th century brought transformation as Bruges encountered a decline. New trade routes and Antwerp's ascent as a trade hub eroded Bruges' cloth trade dominance. However, the 19th century heralded a renaissance. The Romantic Movement's infatuation with medieval allure revitalized Bruges. Its historical charisma lured artists, writers, and tourists, reviving interest in its heritage.

Bruges Today
Present-day Bruges is a fusion of medieval charm and contemporary energy. Its historic canals, cobblestone streets, and pristine architecture harmonize effortlessly with modern boutiques, cafes, and restaurants. The city's profound past echoes through museums, churches, and cultural marvels.

VISUAL POINTERS IN THIS BOOK

PHONE LANGUAGE LOCATION HOTEL TIPS RESTAURANT

LANGUAGE AND PHRASES

The Flemish region of Belgium has its own dialect of Dutch, commonly called "Flemish." While not everyone in Flanders speaks English, most individuals involved in the tourism industry are proficient in it. Flemish television regularly broadcasts English-language programs with Dutch subtitles due to the limited market for dubbing into Dutch. Additionally, speaking French in Flanders may be perceived as insensitive due to historical tensions. It's important to note that place names in Flanders are always given in Dutch, even if the location is actually in France.

ESSENTIAL PHRASES

Greetings

Good morning – Goedemorgen (khoo-duh-mawr-ghuh)
Good day – Goedemiddag (khoo-duh-mih-dahkh)
Good evening – Goedenavond (khoo-duh-nah-fohnt)
Good night – Goedenacht (khoo-duh-nahkht)
Hi / Bye – Hoi / Hallo / Daag / Doei (hoy / hah-loh / dahk / doo-ee)
Goodbye – Tot ziens (toht zeens)

See you next time (in the same day) – Tot straks (toht straks)
See you again – Tot zo (toht zoh)

Common Phrases
Please – Alstublieft (ahlst-ew-bleeft)
Thank you – Dank u wel / Dank je wel (dahnk-ew-vehl / dahnk-yuh-vehl)
Thank you very much – Hartelijk bedankt (hahr-tuh-lik buh-dahnkt)
You're welcome – Graag gedaan (khrahkh khuh-dahn)
I'm sorry – Sorry (saw-ree)
Pardon me – Pardon, wat zei u? (pahr-dohn, vat zay ew)
Yes – Ja (yah)
No – Nee (nay)
How are you? (formal) – Hoe gaat het met u? (hoo khaht ut meht ew)
How are you? (informal) – Hoe gaat het? (hoo khaht ut)

Common Questions
What's your name? (formal) – Hoe heet u? (hoo hayt ew)
What's your name? (informal) – Hoe heet je? (hoo hayt yuh)
My name is... – Ik heet... (ik hayt...)
I am... – Ik ben... (ik ben...)
Nice to meet you. – Aangenaam (ken-nis tuh mah-kuh)
Mister / Misses / Miss – meneer / mevrouw / mejuffrouw (muh-nayr / muh-frow / muh-yuh-frow)
Where are you from? (formal) – Waar komt u vandaan? (vahr kawmt ew fun-dahn)

Where are you from? (informal) – Waar kom je vandaan? (vahr kawn yuh fun-dahn)
I am from the Netherlands. – Ik kom uit Nederland. (ik kawm owt nay-der-lant)
Where do you live? (formal) – Waar woont u? (vahr vohnt ew)
Where do you live? (informal) – Waar woon je? (vahr vohn yuh)
I live in America. – Ik woon in Amerika. (ik vohn in ah-meh-ree-kah)
How old are you? (formal) – Hoe oud bent u? (hoo owt bent ew)
How old are you? (informal) – Hoe oud ben je? (hoo owt ben yuh)
I am _____ years old. – Ik ben ... jaar (oud). (ik ben ... yahr owt)
Do you speak Dutch? (formal) – Spreekt u Nederlands? (spraykt ew nay-der-lahnds)
Do you speak English? (informal) – Spreek je Engels? (sprayk yuh ehng-uhls)

Restaurant Basics
A table for one person/two people, please. – Een tafel voor een/twee alstublieft. (uhn TAH-fuhl vore ane/tway ALS-tuu-bleeft)
Can I look at the menu, please? – Mag ik het menu, alstublieft? (magh ick hut muh-NUU ALS-tuu-bleeft)
Breakfast – ontbijt (ont-BAIYT)
Lunch – Lunch (lunch)
Supper – avondeten (AH-vunt-ay-tun)

I want _____. – Ik wil _____. (ick wil ____)

Basic Numbers
0 – nul (nuhl)
1 – één (ayn)
2 – twee (tyay)
3 – drie (dree)
4 – vier (feer)
5 – vijf (fayf)
6 – zes (zes)
7 – zeven (zay-fern)
8 – acht (akht)
9 – negen (nay-khern)
10 – tien (teen)

Days Of the Week
Monday – maandag (maan-dakh)
Tuesday – dinsdag (dins-dakh)
Wednesday – woensdag (voons-dakh)
Thursday – donderdag (don-der-dakh)
Friday – vrijdag (fray-dakh)
Saturday – zaterdag (zaa-ter-dakh)
Sunday – zondag (zon-dakh)

Months Of the Year
January – Januari (yan-nuw-aa-ree)
February – Februari (fay-bruw-aa-ree)
March – Maart (maart)
April – April (a-pril)
May – Mei (may)

June – Juni (yuw-nee)
July – Juli (juw-lee)
August – Augustus (ow-khuhs-thus)
September – September (sep-tem-ber)
October – Oktober (ok-toa-ber)
November – November (noa-fem-ber)
December – December (day-sem-ber)

Choosing the Best Time to Visit

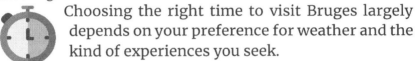
Choosing the right time to visit Bruges largely depends on your preference for weather and the kind of experiences you seek.

April-May: Bruges warms up, signaling the start of spring. Tourist numbers are relatively lower, and the temperature ranges from the 40s to 50s. This period showcases the city adorned with spring flowers and budding greenery. Travelers might also find attractive deals on accommodations during this time. Key events include Meifoor (May) and the Procession of the Holy Blood (May).

June-August: This is when Bruges experiences its warmest weather, with average highs in the low 70s. It's peak tourist season with bustling festivals like Feest in't Park (June), Cactus Festival (July), Moods! (July-August), and Benenwerk (August).

September-October: Early fall sees temperatures drop to the 40s and 50s, and rain becomes more frequent, leading to fewer tourists. It's a great time to visit if you don't mind dressing in layers. Hotel prices tend to decrease after the summer high season, and events like Open Monumentendag (September) are highlights.

November-March: This period brings cold and wet weather, with average lows just above freezing and highs in the mid-40s. However, it offers unique experiences around Christmas and New Year's, featuring events like Winter Glow (November-January) and the Christmas and Winter Market (November-January), with attractions like an ice-skating rink at Minnewaterpark and a festive Christmas market on the Markt.

Each season in Bruges presents a different charm and set of activities, catering to varied preferences and interests.

Travel Essentials

1. Water Filtration Bottle: **Consider carrying a LifeStraw Filtration Water Bottle to enjoy clean, safe drinking water from any source without relying on plastic bottles.**

2. Toiletries Purchase: **Save on luggage space by buying toiletries upon arrival. Major brands are readily available and affordable in Bruges.**

3. Adapters and Converters: **For electrical gadgets, carry a travel adapter plug and a step-down voltage converter if your devices aren't designed for European voltage (230V).**

4. Shoulder Bag or Day Pack: **A comfortable shoulder bag or day pack is essential to carry your sightseeing essentials and keep your hands free.**

5. Luggage Scale: **Avoid unexpected baggage fees by using an accurate luggage scale to stay within weight limits. Keep room for souvenirs—lace from Brussels and Belgian chocolates are must-buys.**

Packing for Weather: **Pack accordingly for variable weather:**

- Spring and Fall: Pack a lightweight raincoat and a travel umbrella for cool and wet weather.
- Summer: Be prepared for rain despite the season.
- Layering: Opt for layers to manage temperature changes—jacket, sweater, shirt, and t-shirt.

- Winter: Dress warmly with layers, a smart coat, scarf, and gloves.

Weather+ App: Consider using the Weather+ app for an accurate 6-day forecast, aiding in planning and keeping track of places visited throughout your trip. Download for iPad/iPhone or Android.

Map of Brugge

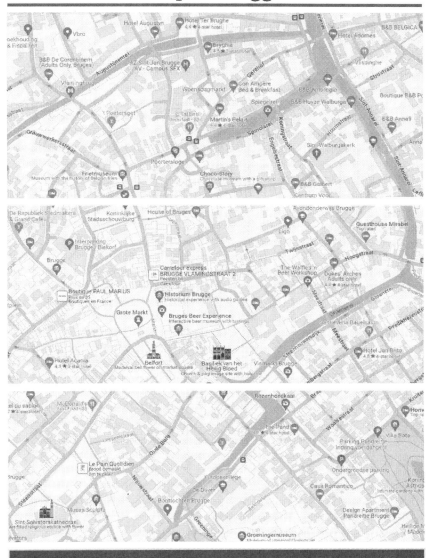

CHAPTER 2

Getting Around

On Foot: The city's small size makes walking the best way to explore. Consider guided tours by the tourism office or reputable companies like Legends Free Walking Tours. Sensible footwear is recommended for the cobblestone streets.

Bicycle: Many accommodations offer bikes, or you can rent one from places like Bruges Bike Rental. Prices start at 4 euros per hour or 13 euros for a day. Bike tours are also available through companies like QuasiMundo and Pink Bear Bike Tours.

Getting to Bruges

Plane: Brussels Airport (BRU) is the closest major airport. From there, a 90-minute train ride brings you to Bruges for about 21 euros.

Train: Belgium's excellent rail network offers direct services to Brussels every 30 minutes. Booking ahead is advised, especially during busy times.

Car: Bruges is well-connected by roads, such as the E40 to Dunkirk and Ghent, the N50 to France and Lille, and the E34 to Antwerp.

Bus: Bus services connect Bruges to various European cities like London and Paris. Tickets from London start at EUR30 with a journey time of 7.5 hours, while fares from Paris begin at EUR12. In Belgium, De Lijn operates a good bus network.

💡 Train Booking: During peak times, especially summer and rush hours, it's advisable to book train tickets in advance.

Car Usage: While the road network is good, driving within Bruges itself can be challenging due to narrow streets.

Bruges' small size and pedestrian-friendly layout make it easy to navigate by foot or bike, offering a charming and accessible travel experience.

Culture & Customs

Once a focal point for artists of the Flemish Primitive painting style, Bruges places art at its core. The city boasts numerous museums, churches, convents, and even a medieval hospital, each housing an impressive collection of artworks. When visiting, ensure you have euros as the local currency. While dining, tipping may not be necessary, as it is typically included in the restaurant bill, with restaurant workers enjoying better compensation compared to the U.S. Leaving a few euros for exceptional service is acceptable but generally not exceeding 10% of the bill. In Bruges, the locals predominantly speak Flemish, but many are proficient in English.

Tips for Travelers

*Plan your trip meticulously. Despite its size, Bruges offers a wealth of attractions, making careful planning essential. Prioritize the attractions you wish to visit, and consider booking tickets in advance.

*Embrace walking or biking. Bruges is highly walkable, providing the best way to explore and absorb its atmosphere. For a more energetic experience, consider renting a bike to traverse the city on two wheels.

*Embark on a canal cruise. One of the most enchanting ways to discover Bruges is through a canal cruise. This offers a unique perspective of the city, coupled with insightful information about its history.

*Visit Markt Square. At the heart of Bruges, Markt Square is perfect for people-watching and immersing yourself in the ambiance. The square hosts numerous restaurants and cafes, making it an ideal spot for a refreshing drink or a bite to eat.

*Ascend the Belfry. The 83-meter-tall Belfry tower provides breathtaking views of the city. While the climb may be a bit challenging, the panoramic views make it worthwhile.

*Indulge in local cuisine. Bruges is a culinary haven, offering a variety of delectable local dishes. Be sure to savor Belgian chocolate, waffles, and frites (fries).

*Experience the nightlife. Bruges boasts a lively nightlife scene, featuring an array of bars and clubs catering to different preferences. Whether you seek a quiet drink or a night out, Bruges has something for everyone.

*Anticipate crowds. As a popular tourist destination, Bruges can get crowded, especially during the summer. If visiting during peak seasons, be prepared for crowds and secure accommodations in advance.

*Pack for diverse weather. Bruges weather can be unpredictable, so pack accordingly. Bring an umbrella, raincoat, and warm clothing, even during the summer months.

*Relax and savor your time in Bruges. With its picturesque charm, Bruges offers a delightful experience. Take your time exploring the city, and feel free to lose yourself in its enchanting streets.

CHAPTER 3

Top Attractions in Bruges

I. Rozenhoedkaai

Considered one of the most photographed areas of Bruges, Rozenhoedkaai, or Quay of the Rosary, is a picturesque spot where the Dijver and Groenerei canals meet. Enjoy the view of lovely canals, beautiful old buildings, and charming bars, restaurants, and hotels.

💡 Best visited during the evening for a magical atmosphere. It's a great starting point for a canal tour.

Price and hours: Free access 24/7; canal boat tours require tickets.

📍 Bruges historic city center, near attractions like Choco-Story and the Groeningemuseum.

II. Historic Centre of Brugge

A UNESCO World Heritage Site since 2000, the Historic Centre of Brugge is a well-preserved medieval European settlement. Explore cobblestone paths, take a boat ride through canals, and admire Gothic and neo-Gothic buildings.

Spend two to three hours in the area, take a canal boat ride, and enjoy a pint of beer and a waffle.

Price and hours: Free.

📍 Location: Center of Bruges.

III. Markt

The heart of Bruges, Markt, is a bustling square filled with shops, cafes, and architecturally interesting buildings like the Belfry. A starting point for exploring Bruges.

💡 Can be crowded; a good starting point for exploration.

📍 Historic city center.
Price and hours: Free

IV. Gruuthusemuseum Bruges

This museum showcases over 500 years of Bruges history through historical artifacts, including tapestries, furniture, coins, and musical instruments.

💡 Highlights include an 18th-century guillotine and a medieval chapel.

📍 Dijver 17c.

Price and hours: Tickets cost 12 euros for adults, free for children 16 and younger. Open Tuesday through Sunday from 9:30 a.m. to 5 p.m.

V. Church of Our Lady

A key structure in the Bruges skyline, the Church of Our Lady features the second-highest brick tower globally and houses Michelangelo's Madonna and Child sculpture.

💡 Impressive artwork and architecture; be aware of possible scaffolding due to renovations.

📍 Rue Mariastraat, less than half a mile south of the Markt.

Price and hours: Church visit is free; 6 euros to view artworks. Open Monday through Saturday from 9:30 a.m. to 5 p.m. and Sunday from 1:30 p.m. to 5 p.m.

VI. Belfry

Dating back to the 13th century, the Belfry stands at 272 feet and offers a climb of 366 stairs to reach panoramic views of Bruges. Housing a carillon with over 40 bells, it's a UNESCO World Heritage-listed building and one of the oldest examples of medieval urban architecture.

💡 The climb offers breathtaking views, but be prepared for potential wait times, especially in the afternoons. Mornings usually have shorter queues.

Cost and Hours: Adults pay 12 euros, youths (6 to 25) pay 10 euros, free for kids under 5 and Musea Brugge Cardholders. Open daily from 9:30 a.m. to 6 p.m.

📍 Markt 7

VII. Minnewater Lake

Located south of central Bruges, Minnewater Lake is a romantic spot, associated with a local legend about eternal love. The area offers benches for serene views and relaxation, complemented by swans that enhance the romantic ambiance.

💡 Beautiful in autumn and less crowded; accessible free of charge.

Access: Best reached by taxi, bike, or walking.

VIII. Beguinage

This site, a UNESCO World Heritage Site, was home to holy laywomen known as beguines in the 1200s. Now inhabited by nuns and a few local unmarried women, it features whitewashed houses and peaceful gardens. The Beguine's house, now a museum, provides insights into 13th-century life.

💡 Visitors can experience a tranquil atmosphere and may hear the nuns singing around noon.

Hours: Open daily from 6:30 a.m. to 6:30 p.m.; the house museum operates from 10 a.m. to 5 p.m. Entrance to the area is free, museum tickets range from free to 2 euros.
📍 Wijngaardstraat

Must-see Activities
1. Boat tour on the canals

I. Boottochten Brugge

Boottochten Brugge offers open-top boat canal tours from Nieuwstraat 11, 8000 Brugge, Belgium, providing commentary and views of medieval landmarks. They operate Mon-Sun from 9:00 AM to 5:00 PM.
☎ +3250333293.

II. City Tour Belgium

Private Brussels Tour with a Local, Custom, Highlights & Hidden Gems
City Tour Belgium provides personalized private tours in Brussels with a local guide. This tour offers flexibility, allowing visitors to explore both popular and lesser-known attractions according to their interests. The price starts from $107.82. The meeting point is at Starbucks, Grand Place 4, 1000 Bruxelles, Belgium, and the tour concludes at the same location.
Book ☏ +1 (702) 648-5873.

Bruges Day Trip from Amsterdam
Embark on a captivating English-language group tour from Brussels to the vibrant and historically rich city of

Amsterdam. Delve into the tales of Amsterdam's key landmarks, including the 13th-century Dam Square and the charming Waag district. With ample free time to explore the city at your own pace, this full-day tour offers a semi-independent experience. Enjoy the convenience of a central Brussels departure. The tour, priced from $63.48.
Book ☎ +1 (702) 648-5873.

📍 Carrefour de l'Europe, Carr de l'Europe, 1000 Bruxelles, Belgium
Start Time: 08:00 AM
End Point: The activity finishes back at the designated meeting spot.

2. Boats of Bruges

For around £10 to £11, enjoy a 30–40-minute boat trip along the scenic waterways with a lively commentary highlighting key sights. This informative tour injects humor into the narration, offering a delightful experience. It serves as a fantastic orientation, allowing you to familiarize yourself with the area for a more detailed exploration later. The route showcases charming and historically significant buildings. Various boarding points offer the same route, making it a highly recommended activity.

📍 Huidenvettersplein 13, Brugge, Belgium

Note: Prices may vary depending on the time of day or season. Please contact the boat companies directly for the most current information.

3. Harbor Tour Zeebruges

Embark on an exploration of an active international port! Immerse yourself in the maritime atmosphere and witness the bustling harbor—cargo ships, ferries, cruise liners, fishing vessels, yachts, and more—all within arm's reach. The tour passes by the Belgian Navy base, gas and wind turbines, the stern island, and one of the world's largest locks. The journey lasts 75 minutes, promising an unforgettable boat trip.

Operating Hours:
Wednesday to Sunday:
10 AM – 12 PM, 2 PM – 5 PM

📍 Tijdokstraat, 8380 Zeebrugge, Belgium
☎ +32597062094

4. Boottochten Stael

A must-visit experience in Bruges! The tour lasts approximately 35-40 minutes, but be prepared for potential wait times in line. It offers a unique and captivating perspective of the city. Morning tours, starting from 10 am onwards, are recommended for the first available slots. The guide delivers information in multiple languages based on passengers' preferences. Note that seating arrangements may not adhere to social distancing guidelines.

Departures and arrivals take place at the same address 📍 Bootexcursies Gruuthuse, boarding point 3, Nieuwstraat 11, 8000 Bruges.
Operating Hours: Monday to Sunday 10:00 AM - 5:00 PM
☎ +3250332771

CHAPTER 4

HOTELS

1. Hotel Relais Bourgondisch Cruyce

A boutique hotel exuding romance, nestled in an extraordinary waterfront residence. Situated along Bruges' historic and picturesque canals, this luxurious abode resides in close proximity to major attractions. Dating back to the 16th century, the hotel showcases exquisite decor with precious antiques, exclusive artwork, and stunning floral arrangements. Its 16 guestrooms, each uniquely designed, boast lavish furnishings including fine antiques, Persian carpets, Ralph Lauren fabrics, and marble bathrooms.

📍 Wollestraat 41 - 47, Bruges 8000, Belgium
☎ Phone: 009 32 50 33 79 26

Facilities
Breakfast buffet, Room service for breakfast, Complimentary tea and wine/champagne, Concierge services, Smoke-free environment, Umbrella provision, Express check-in/check-out, Paid private parking nearby, Free High-Speed Internet (WiFi), 24-hour security and front desk, Baggage storage, Parking garage, Taxi service

Room Amenities
Clothes rack, Private bathrooms, Wake-up service/alarm clock, Flat-screen TV, Bath/shower, Complimentary toiletries, Hairdryer, Allergy-free rooms, Soundproof rooms, Air conditioning, Work desk, Daily housekeeping, Safe, Cable/satellite TV, Walk-in shower, Bathrobes, Telephone, Wardrobe/closet, Bottled water,

Room Options
City view, Landmark view, Non-smoking rooms

 English, French, Dutch

Price:
1 night, 2 adults: US$251
Additional taxes and charges: +US$9

2. Hotel Dukes' Palace Residence

Situated a brief 6-minute stroll from the vibrant Markt Square, this relaxed hotel is conveniently located within a 5-minute walk from the medieval Belfry of Bruges and just 8 minutes away from the Gothic Church of Our Lady Bruges.

Elegantly appointed rooms provide complimentary Wi-Fi, flat-screen TVs, safes, minibars, and facilities for tea and coffee. Upgraded accommodations offer indulgent whirlpool tubs. The hotel amenities feature a stylish bar and versatile meeting spaces. Guests can avail themselves of the breakfast buffet offered for an additional fee.

📍 Ontvangersstraat 9, Bruges 8000, Belgium
☎ +32 50 34 26 90

Property Amenities
On-site paid private parking, Free High-Speed Internet (WiFi), On-site restaurant, Children's television networks, Highchairs available, Taxi service, Business Center with Internet Access, Baggage storage, Secured parking, Breakfast buffet, Complimentary Instant Coffee and tea, Concierge services, Currency exchange, Newspapers, Smoke-free environment, First aid kit, Umbrella provision

Room Features
Soundproof rooms, Bathrobes, Air conditioning, Work desk, Daily housekeeping, Minibar, Cable/satellite TV, Bath/shower, Safe, Seating area, Telephone, Wardrobe/closet, Bottled water, Iron, Refrigerator, Flatscreen TV, Complimentary toiletries, Hairdryer

Room Types
Non-smoking rooms

 German, English, Spanish, French, Dutch

Price: US$153
Additional taxes and charges: +US$16 (as per booking website)

Note:

The property operates under the management of the 5-star Hotel Dukes' Palace, situated in the immediate vicinity. Guests can check in and out at Hotel Dukes' Palace and access all the facilities, including the bar, restaurant, lounge, and concierge.

3. Relais & Chateaux Hotel Heritage

Situated just 2 km from Brugge's main rail terminal, this sophisticated hotel resides in an elegant 19th-century building. It's conveniently a mere 2 minutes' walk from Grote Markt square and a short 3-minute stroll from the medieval Belfry of Bruges.

Niklaas Desparsstraat 11, 8000 Brugge, Belgium
+32 50 44 44 44 / 009 32 4 268 05 44

Nestled discreetly in the historical city center, this enchanting 5-star Boutique Hotel is the exclusive Relais & Chateaux member in Bruges. Within walking distance are the city's most coveted attractions, premium boutiques, and gourmet dining venues, including landmarks like the Belfry Tower, the Church of Our Lady, the Basilica of the Holy Blood, and historic museums. Isabelle and Johan Creytens, the proud proprietors, along with their dedicated team, extend a warm welcome to guests, ensuring an unforgettable experience. Indulge in Chef Gregory Slembrouck's culinary masterpieces at the onsite award-winning restaurant, Le Mystique, or luxuriate in the spa's pampering services, featuring massages, sauna, and steam baths at "Le Moment by Sothys."

Property Amenities
Electric vehicle charging station, Free High-Speed Internet (WiFi), Fitness Center with Gym/Workout Room, Bar/lounge, Car hire services, Foot bath, 24-hour security, Baggage storage, Valet parking, on-site paid private parking, Sauna, Restaurant, Breakfast available, Breakfast buffet, In-room coffee amenities, Wine/champagne service, Taxi service, Foot massage facilities

Room Features
Allergy-free rooms, Blackout curtains, Air conditioning, Desk, Fireplace, Coffee/tea maker, Cable/satellite TV, Bath/shower, Soundproof rooms, Air purifier, Bathrobes, Housekeeping, Room service, Safe, Sofa, Telephone, VIP

room facilities, Wardrobe/closet, Bottled water, Clothes rack

Room Types
City view, Landmark view, Non-smoking rooms, Suites, Bridal suite

Price:
1 night, 2 adults: US$360

Additional taxes and charges: +US$9

4. Hotel de Orangerie

Nestled along the Den Dijver canal, this refined hotel occupies a grand 15th-century former convent. It's a mere 3-minute walk from Markt square and just 7 minutes on foot from Choco Story, The Chocolate Museum.

Kartuizerinnenstraat 10, 8000 Brugge, Belgium
+32 50 34 16 49

Hotel de Orangerie rests along the most picturesque canal in medieval Bruges, right at the heart of the city center. This converted XV century monastery of the Sisters Karthuizerinnen has been transformed into an exquisite "boutique hotel," adorned with exclusive fabrics and antiques. Each of the 20 graciously appointed bedrooms is individually adorned with antiques, offering the modern comforts expected by discerning travelers. The elegant Salon, situated alongside the canal, invites guests to unwind by the open fire, ensconced in comfortable sofas while perusing available art books and international magazines, and enjoying round-the-clock drink service. Guests are encouraged to savor the typical English "Afternoon Tea" or an aperitif on the waterfront terrace or within the cozy and enchanting breakfast room.

Elegantly designed rooms reflect French Country style, each uniquely furnished, and equipped with free Wi-Fi, flat-screen TVs, minibars, Nespresso machines, and designer toiletries. Some rooms offer canal views, while suites feature living areas, some including sofa beds. 24/7 room service is available.

The hotel features an antiquity-filled bar complete with a fireplace. Continental breakfast and afternoon tea (additional cost) are served in a charming old-world dining room or on a terrace with scenic canal views. Parking options are provided nearby.

Room Types
City view, Non-smoking rooms, Suites, Family rooms, Bridal suite

 German, English, French, Dutch

Price: 1 NIGHT, 2 ADULTS: US$286
Additional taxes and charges: +US$9

5. The Pand Hotel

The Pand Hotel, recognized by the Tatler Guide as one of the 101 best in the world, is a member of Small Luxury Hotels of The World. It occupies an 18th-century carriage house, exquisitely adorned with antiques, objets d'art, and Ralph Lauren fabrics. Situated just around the corner from the Market Square, it's only 35 meters away from the famous Dijver quay and the canals.

📍 Pandreitje 16, Bruges 8000 Belgium

The hotel provides 26 rooms offering modern comforts, luxurious bathrooms, free Wi-Fi, air conditioning, and flat-screen TVs. The lavish breakfast, served with a champagne touch and waiter service, takes place in the breakfast room, where eggs are freshly prepared on granny's stove.

Guests can unwind in the bar or library by the fireplace, admiring the collection of old books and Louis Vuitton suitcases. Amenities include a 24-hour reception, private garage, and an exclusive limousine service. The Groeningemuseum is just 250 meters away, while the Rozenhoedkaai offers a scenic view right outside the hotel. Bruges Railway Station is a leisurely 15-minute walk.

Room Types
City view, Bridal suite, Non-smoking rooms, Suites

 English, French, Spanish, Dutch, German, Portuguese

Price:
1 NIGHT, 2 ADULTS: US$236

Additional taxes and charges: +US$9

6. Hotel Van Cleef

🏨 Hotel Van Cleef is housed in a grand Italianate mansion on one of Bruges' stunning canals. This small luxury boutique hotel combines classical and contemporary styles, offering top-notch facilities with traditional service standards.

📍 Molenmeers 11, Bruges 8000 Belgium
☎ 009 32 50 34 64 14

The hotel boasts luxurious air-conditioned suites featuring spa baths, flat-screen TVs, and free Wi-Fi. Each suite has boutique-style décor, extra-long beds, and a comfortable seating area with a minibar.

Within a 5-minute walk from the main shopping streets and just 750 meters from the Groeninge Museum, Hotel Van Cleef is conveniently located. Guests can unwind in the library or opt for a relaxing massage. Additionally, the hotel offers bicycle rental services and a tour desk for local tourist information and tickets.

Property Amenities
Paid private parking on-site, Free High-Speed Internet (WiFi), Bar/lounge, Strollers, Baggage storage, Concierge, 24-hour front desk, Private check-in/check-out, Wifi, Breakfast available, Breakfast in the room, Special diet menus, Gift shop, Newspaper, Non-smoking hotel, Shared lounge/TV area, Shops, Sun terrace, Dry cleaning, Laundry service, Ironing service, Shoeshine

Room Features
Allergy-free room, Soundproof rooms, Air conditioning, Housekeeping, Private balcony, Safe, Minibar, Flatscreen TV, Bathrobes, VIP room facilities, Bottled water, Wake-up service/alarm clock

Room Types
Bridal suite, Non-smoking rooms, Suites, Family rooms

 English, French, Spanish, Dutch, German, Italian

Price:
1 NIGHT, 2 ADULTS: US$370
Additional taxes and charges: +US$9

RESTAURANTS
1. That's Toast!

That's Toast! offers an all-day breakfast and toast bar experience, serving barista coffees, freshly made cold-pressed juices, and a diverse selection of hearty and sweet toasts, grains, fruits, and full breakfast plates. Guests can enjoy the vibrant atmosphere for an affordable sit-down meal or opt to take their products to go. The restaurant does not take reservations.

Dweersstraat 4, Bruges 8000 Belgium
+32 50 68 82 27

Price Range:
$4 - $15
Cuisines:
Cafe, International, European, Fusion, Healthy
Special Diets:
Vegetarian Friendly, Vegan Options, Gluten Free Options
Meals:
Breakfast, Lunch, Brunch, Drinks
Features:
Gift Cards Available, Outdoor Seating, Seating, Highchairs Available, Wheelchair Accessible, Serves Alcohol (Wine and Beer), Digital Payments, Free Wifi, Accepts Credit Cards, Table Service, Dog Friendly
Hours:
Sunday to Saturday: 08:30 AM - 4:00 PM

2. Tante Marie

Tante Marie is situated in the historic Broussard Hardware building in downtown Breaux Bridge. It's a space cherished by local artists and musicians, offering a variety of Belgian, European, and international cuisines along with coffees, specialty cocktails, wine, and beer.

Kerkstraat 38, Damme 8340 Belgium
+32 50 35 45 03

Cuisines:
Belgian, European, International
Special Diets:
Vegetarian Friendly, Vegan Options, Gluten Free Options
Meals:
Lunch, Dinner, Brunch, Drinks
Features:
Reservations, Outdoor Seating, Seating, Free Wifi, Accepts Credit Cards, Table Service, Highchairs Available, Wheelchair Accessible, Serves Alcohol
Hours:
Sunday to Friday: 10:00 AM - 6:00 PM

3. Grill Restaurant Passie

Grill Restaurant Passie resides in a charming old building in the heart of Bruges, offering a stylish and modern interior with a warm and inviting atmosphere. Its outdoor terrace provides a delightful setting for enjoying a meal, especially on warm summer days. The menu boasts a diverse array of grilled meats, including steaks, chops, and burgers, alongside tempting seafood options like grilled fish, lobster, and shrimp. Complementing these are a variety of salads, appetizers, and desserts. The restaurant's service is excellent, with friendly and attentive staff always willing to recommend dishes and assist with queries. Grill Restaurant Passie is perfect for a romantic dinner, special occasions, or a night out with friends, offering delicious meals in a beautiful setting.

Nieuwstraat 83, 4524 EG Sluis, The Netherlands
0117712630

Price Range:
$11 - $44
Cuisines:
Dutch, International, Barbecue, Grill
Special Diets:
Vegetarian Friendly, Gluten Free Options
Meals:
Lunch, Dinner, Brunch
Features:
Outdoor Seating, Seating, Parking Available (Free off-street parking), Highchairs Available, Wheelchair

Accessible, Serves Alcohol, Full Bar, Free Wifi, Reservations, Accepts Visa, Accepts Credit Cards, Table Service, Validated Parking, Accepts Mastercard,
Hours:
Sunday to Saturday: 12:00 PM - 3:00 PM, 5:00 PM - 8:00 PM

4. At Tattie's

At Tattie's is a charming and cozy restaurant in Bruges, Belgium, celebrated for its delectable Belgian cuisine, warm hospitality, and inviting ambiance. Nestled amid the picturesque canals and medieval architecture of Bruges, At Tattie's offers an authentic taste of Belgian culinary delights. Their menu showcases culinary gems prepared with fresh, locally sourced ingredients and a dedication to traditional cooking methods. From hearty stews and savory meat dishes to fresh seafood and enticing vegetarian options, At Tattie's caters to a wide range of palates.

Jan van Eyckplein 3, Bruges 8000 Belgium

+32 50 69 29 54

Price Range:
$3 - $24
Cuisines:
Belgian, Cafe, European, Healthy
Special Diets:
Vegetarian Friendly, Gluten Free Options, Vegan Options
Meals:
Breakfast, Lunch, Brunch
Features:
Takeout, Outdoor Seating, Seating, Table Service, Serves Alcohol, Free Wifi, Accepts Credit Cards
Hours:
Monday to Saturday: 08:00 AM - 3:30 PM

5. 'T Koetshuis

'T Koetshuis offers delicious food, prompt and friendly service, and a diverse range of drinks. Located beside the historic Ravenhof castle where Count Moretus once resided, the restaurant serves both lunch and dinner. In the summer, guests can enjoy the outdoor seating and watch the world go by. It's an ideal spot for a leisurely walk or cycle, exploring the beautiful gardens and woods.

Oud Broek 2, Stabroek 2940 Belgium
+32 3 605 84 85

Price Range:
US$4 - US$27
Cuisines:
Belgian, European, French, Bar, Pub, Diner, Healthy
Special Diets:
Suitable for vegetarians
Meals:
Lunch, Dinner, Drinks, Brunch
Functions:
Reservations, Seating, Parking Available (Street Parking, Free Off-Street Parking), Wheelchair Accessible, Outdoor Seating, Validated Parking, Highchairs Available, Full Bar, Wine and Beer, Digital Payments, Free Wifi, Accepts Credit Cards, Table Service, Delivery, Serves Alcohol
Opening Hours:
Monday-Saturday: 10:00 AM - 10:00 PM

6. de Verbeelding

De Verbeelding serves delicious food with well-proportioned dishes delivered at a thoughtful pace. The menu, though not extensive, offers a mix of classic tapas and local dishes prepared in a "tapas" style. Highlights include the tasty kibbeling and the crispy chicken with an unexpected and intriguing coating.

Price Range:
$10 - $26
Cuisines:
Belgian, European
Special Diets:
Vegetarian Friendly, Gluten Free Options, Vegan Options

◉ Meals:
Lunch, Dinner, Brunch, Late Night, Drinks
Features:
Reservations, Seating, Highchairs Available, Wheelchair Accessible, Table Service, Wine and Beer, Accepts Mastercard, Serves Alcohol, Full Bar, Free Wifi, Accepts Credit Cards, Accepts Visa, Family style, Gift Cards Available
Hours:
Tuesday-Saturday: 5:00 PM - 11:00 PM

Oude Burg 26, Bruges 8000 Belgium
☏ +32 498 45 89 74

CHAPTER 5

Top Perfect Souvenirs in Bruges

Bruges, a city with a rich history and vibrant marketplaces, offers an array of delightful souvenirs for every traveler. Here are eight perfect keepsakes to bring home from your visit:

Christmas Ornaments

Experience the enchantment of Christmas year-round by exploring specialty shops for beautiful ornaments and decorations. **De Witte Pelikaan** on Vlamingstraat 23 offers a magical selection with elegant chandeliers and twinkling lights.

📍 Vlamingstraat 23, Bruges 8000 Belgium
Open Hours: Monday-Sunday 10:00 AM - 5:30 PM

Flemish Tapestries

Explore the craft of tapestry-making, a tradition dating back to the Middle Ages. **Mille Fleurs** on Wollestraat 18 presents a collection of wall-hangings, pillow covers, and handbags featuring detailed and colorful images, including scenes of old cities, flowers, and landscapes.

- Wollestraat 18, Bruges 8000 Belgium
  Open Hours: Monday-Sunday 10:00 AM - 6:00 PM

Comic Books

Dive into the world of comics, with a special nod to the beloved Adventures of Tintin series originating from Belgium. **De Striep** on Katelijnestraat 42 offers a fantastic collection of comic books and memorabilia in various languages.

- Katelijnestraat 42, Bruges 8000 Belgium
  Open Hours: Monday-Saturday 1:30 PM - 7:00 PM

Chocolates

A journey to Belgium wouldn't be fully experienced without delighting in its renowned and globally acclaimed chocolates. Dumon, a family-run artisanal chocolate shop near Markt square, and Chocolate Line, known for innovative chocolate creations, are must-visit destinations. Explore the history of Belgian chocolate at the **Chocolate Museum (Choco Story)** on Wijnzakstraat 2.

Simon Stevinplein 19, Bruges 8000 Belgium

Open Hours:
Monday: 10:30 AM - 6:30 PM
Tuesday-Saturday: 9:30 AM - 6:30 PM
Sunday: 10:30 AM - 6:30 PM

Antiques

De Clerck Antiques: Discover antique furniture, glassware, and ceramics meticulously curated by the family owners.

📍 Walplein 12, Bruges 8000 Belgium
Opening Hours: Monday-Saturday 10:00 AM - 7:00 PM

Cheese

Diksmuids Boterhuis: Over 200 varieties of cheese await, offering tasting tours to explore the cheese-making process and indulge in a delightful goodie bag.

Geldmuntstraat 23, Bruges 8000 Belgium
 +32 50 33 32 43

Sweets

Confiserie De Clerck: Delight in traditional sweets like caramelized chew, spekke, in a centuries-old family-run shop.

Confiserie Zucchero: Watch colorful confections being made on-site in this artisan candy shop.

Academiestraat 19, 8000 Brugge

Lace

'T Apostelientje: Specializes in antique and handmade lace, offering intricate and delicate pieces.

Lace Center: Discover lace-making students crafting their latest creations alongside lace fabrics.

Balstraat 11, Bruges 8000 Belgium

CHAPTER 6

📍

Must-Visit Events in Bruges

1. Moods! Festival

Dates: July 12-14, 2024

The Moods! Festival, previously known as Klinkers, is a city-wide festival revitalizing Bruges in July and August. Over eight concert evenings, it offers diverse and relevant sounds against the picturesque medieval backdrop of Bruges. Free of charge, it's a vibrant celebration of music and culture.

Minnewaterpark, Brugge, Belgium

 +32 50 33 20 14

2. Feest in het Park

Date: Second weekend of July

(Party in the Park) An annual family festival that transforms the Minnewaterpark into a lively celebration. The event includes performances by various artists and bands, offering a fun-filled experience amidst warm, bright summer days.

Minnewaterpark, Brugge, Belgium

3. Brugse Meifoor (Bruges May Fair)
📍 Brugse Meifoor is the city's largest fair, featuring around 90 attractions. It runs for approximately a month, commencing on the third Friday after Easter and concluding the weekend after Ascension Day. The fair kicks off with a children's costumed procession and fireworks. The Friday after Ascension Day marks a traditional reduced-price day.
't Zand, Brugge, Belgium

4. Kathedraal Festival
📍 St. Salvators Cathedral, Sint-Salvatorskoorstraat 8, 8000 Bruges
Phone Number: 476-75-63-85

This festival promotes organ culture, spotlighting the monumental organ of the Cathedral of San Salvador. Each year, it welcomes different artists for various concerts, emphasizing the beauty and significance of organ music.

Five-Day Itinerary
Day 1: Exploring the Historic Center
Morning: Commence your day by visiting the iconic Belfry of Bruges (Belfort van Brugge) to relish panoramic views of the city. Following this, take a leisurely stroll through the Historic Centre of Bruges (Historisch Centrum van Brugge) and marvel at the breathtaking medieval architecture. Don't forget to explore the Basilica of the

Holy Blood (Heilig-Bloedbasiliek), housing a revered relic.

Afternoon: Head to De Halve Maan Brewery for a guided tour and a tasting session featuring their renowned Brugse Zot beer. Subsequently, immerse yourself in the world of Belgian chocolate by visiting Choco-Story, the Chocolate Museum, to learn about its history and production. Conclude your afternoon with a visit to Market Square (Markt), where you can admire the splendid buildings and savor a snack at a local cafe.

Evening: Treat yourself to a delectable dinner at Le Mystique, a Michelin-starred restaurant celebrated for its innovative cuisine. Afterwards, enjoy a leisurely stroll along the Minnewater (Lake of Love) and soak in the romantic ambiance of this picturesque location.

Bedtime: Discover exceptional hotels in Bruges.

DAY 2: Historical Gems and Beguinage

Morning: Embark on your day by visiting the Church of Our Lady (Onze-Lieve-Vrouwekerk), home to the renowned Madonna and Child sculpture by Michelangelo. Next, explore the Princely Beguinage Ten Wijngaarde (Begijnhof), a serene UNESCO World Heritage site. Don't overlook a visit to Sint-Janshospitaal (Saint John's Hospital), showcasing a captivating collection of art and medical artifacts.

Afternoon: Delight in a relaxed lunch at Burgerij, acclaimed for its gourmet burgers made from locally sourced ingredients. Then, delve into the Groeningemuseum, exhibiting a diverse collection of

Flemish art spanning numerous centuries. Conclude your afternoon with a visit to the Diamond Museum (Diamantmuseum) to discover the history and craftsmanship behind diamonds.

Evening: Immerse yourself in the cozy ambiance of De Vlaamsche Pot, a traditional Flemish restaurant renowned for its hearty cuisine. Following dinner, venture to De Garre, a hidden gem celebrated for its extensive selection of Belgian beers. Enjoy a tranquil and delightful evening in this charming establishment.

Bedtime: Discover exceptional hotels in Bruges.

DAY 3: City Hall and Beer Tasting

Morning: Begin your day by exploring the grandeur of the Bruges City Hall (Stadhuis van Brugge), an imposing Gothic structure nestled in the city's heart. Follow this with a guided walking tour and a relaxing canal boat trip, offering a picturesque view of the city's charming streets and waterways.

Afternoon: Savor a delectable lunch at De Stoepa, a cozy restaurant blending Belgian and Asian cuisines. Afterwards, immerse yourself in the brewing heritage at the Bruges Beer Museum (Brugs Biermuseum). Conclude your afternoon with a beer tasting session at Duvelorium, situated within the historic Belfry building.

Evening: Indulge in a gourmet dining experience at De Karmeliet, a prestigious three-Michelin-starred restaurant celebrated for its exquisite cuisine. Later, unwind at Quatre Mains, a chic cocktail bar, where you can enjoy a nightcap while relishing live music.

Bedtime: Explore exceptional hotels in Bruges for a comfortable stay.

DAY 4: Art and Exploration
Morning: Immerse yourself in art at the Groeningemuseum, showcasing a vast collection of Flemish and Belgian art spanning from the 15th to the 21st century. Then, delve into the medieval ambiance at Historium Brugge, an interactive museum offering a journey back in time to medieval Bruges.
Afternoon: Relax over a delightful lunch at De Republiek, a lively café housed within a former monastery. Embark on a guided rickshaw tour, unveiling the hidden nooks and charming streets of Bruges.
Evening: Enjoy the inviting atmosphere of B'artiest, a cozy restaurant celebrated for its seasonal and locally sourced cuisine. Following dinner, venture to 't Huidevettershuis, a historic bar, to savor traditional Belgian beers.
Bedtime: Discover exceptional hotels in Bruges for a restful evening.

DAY 5: Unique Experiences and Farewell
Morning: Dive into a hands-on experience at the Bruges Belgian Waffle-Making Workshop with Beer Tasting. Master the art of crafting authentic Belgian waffles while relishing a tasting of local beers. Then, venture on a self-guided highlights scavenger hunt and walking tour to uncover hidden gems and lesser-known attractions.

Afternoon: Delight in a leisurely lunch at Quatre Mains, a chic restaurant merging Belgian and international cuisine. Following this, embark on a serene boat cruise along Bruges' canals, soaking in the picturesque views.

Evening: Conclude your journey with a farewell dinner at Tom's Diner, a cozy eatery renowned for its comforting dishes. Cherish the memories forged during your Bruges escapade.

Bedtime: Discover exceptional hotels in Bruges for a serene night's rest.

CHAPTER 7

Safety and Security in Bruges

Safety at Night

Bruges is generally safe for solo female travelers, even at night. Well-lit streets and vibrant nightlife contribute to a secure atmosphere. Public transportation and taxis are readily available, providing alternatives to walking alone. While petty crime can occur, staying cautious and sticking to well-populated areas enhances safety.

Public Transportation

Bruges boasts safe and reliable public transportation. Buses and trains maintain high standards, with easily accessible schedules. Conductors and drivers often communicate in English, ensuring convenience for foreign travelers. Violent incidents on public transport are rare, but travelers should remain vigilant about their surroundings and belongings.

Street Harassment

Known for its peaceful atmosphere, Bruges experiences low instances of street harassment. The locals are generally respectful, and it's considered safe to walk around, even at night. Travelers are advised to stay aware of their surroundings, a good practice anywhere.

Petty Crimes

While petty crimes like pickpocketing occur, Bruges has lower frequencies compared to larger cities. Basic precautions, such as securing belongings, contribute to a safe travel experience.

Tap Water

Tap water in Bruges is safe for drinking, adhering to stringent EU standards. It undergoes rigorous testing and purification, making it as clean, if not cleaner, than bottled water. Tourists can confidently refill their bottles throughout the day.

Laws and Cultural Differences

Personal ID: Carrying identification, such as a passport or national ID card, is a legal requirement.

Laws on Clothing: Wearing clothing that obscures the face is illegal, with potential fines and detention.

Illegal Drugs and Prison Sentences: Drug possession or trafficking can result in a minimum 3-month prison sentence or a fine.

Visiting Battlefields: Caution is advised when visiting WW1 battlefields, with an emphasis on staying on designated paths and reporting any discoveries of potential hazards to the police.

Road Travel

Belgium has a high accident rate, often due to speeding. If driving, it's crucial to adhere to local regulations.

Low emission zones exist in Brussels, Ghent, and Antwerp, requiring pre-registration for foreign vehicles on respective city websites.

Driving Regulations

Driving laws in Belgium differ from those in the UK. Be mindful of speed traps, cameras, and unmarked vehicles used by the police.

Speeding can lead to on-the-spot fines, and using a mobile phone while driving is illegal unless using hands-free equipment.

If fined, consulting the federal justice service for information is advisable.

Required Documents

When driving in Belgium, ensure you have:
1. Driving license
2. Car papers
3. Insurance paper
4. MOT ('contrôle technique') certificate
5. Passport/ID for yourself and passengers

Electric Scooter Regulations

The maximum speed limit for electric scooters is 25km/h, and riding with a passenger is illegal.

Users aged 15 and under are generally prohibited from riding electric scooters, except in designated areas.

Emergency Numbers

The official emergency number is 112, connecting to all emergency services. English-speaking police officers are often available in Belgium's cities.

Language Sensitivity
Belgium is trilingual, speaking French, Flemish, and German. Be mindful of regional language preferences as speaking the wrong language might cause offense. When uncertain, English is often a neutral choice.

Train Travel Caution
On popular international train routes, pickpockets can be active. Keep valuables secure, and consider placing bags at the end of your train corridor for better visibility.

Driving in Brussels
Traffic congestion is common in Brussels, and vehicle theft is prevalent. Consider avoiding driving in the city, if possible, to minimize risks associated with both traffic and theft.

Safety for Women
Women travelers should exercise additional caution due to instances of catcalling and verbal harassment. Being aware of surroundings and taking precautions is advisable.

CONCLUSION

Your journey through Bruges concludes, yet its enchantment lingers, much like the melody of a street musician's violin. The cobblestone streets, once echoing your steps, now hold a treasury of memories, waiting for your return. You've unraveled the rich tapestry of this city, delving into its medieval splendor, uncovering artistic treasures, and tracing its evolution from a trade hub to a modern jewel. Walking in the footsteps of its past, you've witnessed Bruges' transformation through the ages. Bruges has delighted your senses with the aroma of freshly baked waffles, the harmonious bells of its churches, and the sun's golden embrace on its canals. Its distinct character has left an indelible mark on your memories. This city has offered solace to your wandering spirit, whether in solitary strolls through Minnewater Park, romantic carriage rides, or joyful explorations with loved ones. It beckoned you to embrace its unhurried pace and revel in its medieval allure. As you bid adieu, Bruges whispers a promise—a promise of undiscovered treasures, uncharted experiences yet to be embraced. It invites you to return, to rediscover its timeless allure and immerse yourself in the spellbinding charm of a truly extraordinary city.

HAPPY TRAVELLING